MINDFULNESS

MINDFULNESS MADE SIMPLE, FUN, AND CRYSTAL CLEAR

DANIEL ROBBINS

CONTENTS

Introduction   v

1. What is Mindfulness?   1
2. Principles of Mindfulness   5
3. How to Practice Mindfulness   8
4. Steps to Mindfulness   14
5. Obstacles to Mindfulness and How to Overcome Them   24

INTRODUCTION

Mindfulness is the act of centering your consideration on the present and, without being judgmental, watching all parts of your general surroundings and also your musings, sentiments and responses. It is additionally called being aware of your own self. Despite the fact that this sounds so straightforward, it's really not the same as the way that a vast majority of us choose to live our lives. It is important to understand the difference between mindfulness and being oblivious or being overpowered by contemplations of what we have to do, what happened in our past, or what we ought to have done.

We often get perplexed, and we feel like life is slipping away ceaselessly. We accept that life is meaningless and beyond our control. We rush and stress and we're reluctant to back off. By living thusly, we miss the real life that we have been sent on earth to experience. We additionally increase the danger of sickness and damage. Mindful contemplation, or vipassana, is a Buddhist custom created 2,500 years ago to help individuals live every minute of their lives, even the tormenting ones, as completely as possible.

For as far back as 20 years, it has been utilized to reconnect the psyche and the body, especially by pioneers of this field.

Mindfulness is utilized as both contemplation and a practice in ordinary life. Honing mindfulness might be useful to individuals with an extensive variety of sicknesses, and in managing anxiety, frenzy ambushes, and enthusiastic torments. Indeed, it might be utilized by anybody to advance life, to grow the ability to live and adore, to manage life's good and bad times in an agreeable and cool way, and to diminish physical torment.

Studies indicate that in only eight weeks of preparation and mindfulness, the mind and the way it forms feeling under anxiety might be changed. At the end of eight weeks, the insusceptible framework is more vigorous, individuals feel calmer, and they feel better about their bodies. The danger of harm is significantly lessened. Anxiety is an aggregate personality/body reaction to an apparent danger. Reactions originate from envisioned dangers. When we start to live with this awareness, not to our thoughts regarding how things might be, but to life as it truly seems to be, we can give careful consideration to the real dangers and disperse our reasons for alarm. By being mindful, we are conscious to the event, and we can act unmistakably and cleverly to avoid the true dangers.

The anxiety response includes the endocrine and focal sensory systems that discharge anxiety hormones into our bodies. Since life is brimming with turbulence, we are regularly in a state of stress that brings about such physical issues as hypertension, misery, migraines, spinal pains, and sleep deprivation. Stress measurably causes an issue of the musculoskeletal, cardiovascular, nervous, and gastrointestinal frameworks.

Unbending thinking and practices that may have once

kept us safe turn into our foes when our reality perspective is tested. Anything that doesn't fit into our idea of "typical" is alarming and becomes a cause of our stress. To adapt to mental uneasiness, numerous individuals try to stay busy all the time, or they create addictive connections to sex, nourishment, alcohol or medications. Stress undermines the soundness of our brains and our bodies and can conceivably slaughter us. Besides this, it additionally ransacks us of the nature of life.

Mindfulness can be a help to you if –

- Your life's voyage is not an undertaking but an obsessive need to arrive, to achieve, and to "make it."
- You probably won't see the blossoms by the wayside, nor are you mindful of the excellence of life as it unfolds around you.
- You are continually attempting to get some place other than where you are.
- You feel that what you are doing is a necessary chore.
- You are waiting for satisfaction from something or somebody later on.

In this book, we will elaborate on the concept of mindfulness, how to create it, and how to apply it to different parts of your life.

1

WHAT IS MINDFULNESS?

Mindfulness can be described as a mirror-thought. It reflects just what is without further ado, precisely the way it is going on. There are no inclinations. Moreover, mindfulness is a non-judgmental perception. It is that capability of the psyche which is enables you to see without feedback. With this capacity, one sees things without judgment.

One is astonished by nothing. One basically takes an adjusted enthusiasm toward things precisely as they are in their regular states. One does not choose and does not pass judgment. One simply watches. It is beneficial for you to understand that when we say, "One does not choose and does not pass judgment," what we mean is that the meditator watches encounters like a researcher watching an item under a magnifying instrument without any preconceived ideas, just to see the article precisely as it seems to be. In the same way, the meditator notices impermanence, unsuitable quality, and magnanimity.

It is mentally unimaginable for us to watch what is happening inside us dispassionately, in the event that we don't in the meantime acknowledge the different states of the brain. This is particularly true with unsavoury states of psyche. So as to watch our own particular trepidation, we must acknowledge that we are afraid. We can't analyze our own particular sadness without tolerating it completely. The same is valid for aggravation and disturbance, disappointment, and each one of those other uncomfortable passionate states.

You can't analyze something completely in the event that you are occupied with dismissing its presence. Whatever experience you may be having, mindfulness simply acknowledges it. No pride, no disgrace, what is there will be there.

Therefore, in entirety, mindfulness is a fair-minded watchfulness. It doesn't take sides. It doesn't get hung up on what is seen. It simply sees. It doesn't attempt to evade the awful mental states. There is no sticking to the average and no escaping from the unpleasant. Mindfulness treats all encounters just as, all musings similarly, all emotions just as. Nothing is smothered. Nothing is subdued. In other words, there is no prioritizing.

Mindfulness is not considering. It doesn't get included with thought or ideas. It doesn't get hung up on thoughts or suppositions or memories. It simply looks. Mindfulness registers encounters, but it doesn't analyze them. It doesn't name them or arrange them. It simply watches everything as though it was happening surprisingly. It is not an examination that is focused around reflection and memory. It is, fairly, the immediate and quick encountering of whatever is going on, without the medium of thought. It precedes thought in the perceptual procedure.

Mindfulness can also be described as the awareness of the present. It is the recognition of what is going on at this moment. It stays everlastingly in the present, unendingly on the peak of the continuous wave of sitting back. In the event that you are recalling your second-review instructor, that is memory. When you then gotten mindful that you are recollecting your second-review educator, that is being aware. On the off chance that you then conceptualize the methodology and say to yourself, "Goodness, I am recalling," that is considering.

MINDFULNESS IS A FORM OF ALERTNESS, which is non-egoistic in nature. It happens without reference to self. With care one sees all phenomena without references to ideas like "me," "my," or "mine." For instance, assume there is pain in your left leg. Normal cognizance would say, "I have pain." Using mindfulness, one would essentially note the sensation as a sensation. One would not attach that additional idea "I." Mindfulness prevents one from adding anything to discernment, or subtracting anything from the same. One does not upgrade anything. One does not underscore anything. One simply watches precisely what is there—without mutilation.

Mindfulness is consciousness of progress. It is watching the passing stream of experience. It is viewing things as they are evolving. It is seeing the conception, development, and development of all phenomena. It is viewing phenomena maturely and passing on. Moreover, it is viewing things minute by minute, ceaselessly and watching all phenomena — physical, mental, or passionate—that is quickly occurring in the brain. One simply kicks back and watches the show.

Mindfulness is the recognition of the essential nature of each passing wonder. It is viewing the thing emerging and passing ceaselessly. It is, in a way, the process of perceiving how that thing makes us feel and how we respond to it. It is watching how it influences others. In other words, one is an impartial onlooker whose sole occupation is to stay informed.

The meditator who is creating self-awareness is not concerned with the outer universe. It is there, yet in contemplation, one's field of study is one's encounter, one's contemplations, one's sentiments, and one's discernments. In meditation, one will be one's research center. The universe inside has a colossal trust of data holding the impression of the outer world and significantly more. An examination of this prompts complete opportunity.

Mindfulness is participatory perception. The meditator is both member and spectator at one and the same time. On the off chance that one watches one's feelings or physical sensations, one is feeling them at that same minute. Being aware is not an erudite mindfulness. It is simply mindfulness. The mirror-thought illustration breaks down here. It is the attentive knowledge of life, an interest in the continuous methodology of living.

It is extremely difficult to describe mindfulness in words, not on the grounds that it is intricate, but since it is excessively basic and open. The same issue crops up in all aspects of human experience. The most essential idea is dependably the most troublesome to bind. Take a gander at a word reference and you will see an agreeable sample. Long words, for the most part, have compact definitions. However, short essential words like "the" and "be," can have definitions a page long. Also in material science, the most troublesome capacities to depict are the most essential ones that manage the most basic substances of quantum mechanics.

2

PRINCIPLES OF MINDFULNESS

There are two facets of mindfulness namely, mindfulness in regular life and mindful meditation. Both are paramount and important to get the profits of mindfulness. Mindful meditation is altogether different from transcendental contemplation or other comparative practices where you center consideration on one thing and prohibit all different considerations and distractions. Those practices can lead to profound states of smoothness. Mindful meditation starts by centering, to create serenity and soundness. However, then it goes past that state to one of centred consideration.

As opposed to overlooking or stifling contemplations that come into the brain, considerations are noted and watched deliberately without judgment, minute by minute, as events in the field of mindfulness. Today, mindfulness is not generally a religious practice, yet since Buddhists initially created it, there exists the concept of vipassana meditation, which stresses a Buddhist focus. For individuals who are extremely occupied, meditation obliges discipline on the grounds that it includes requiring some investment every day to do practices which will fortify the ability to be mindful in day to day life.

MINDFULNESS in ordinary life is basically minute to-minute mindfulness, so any movement is an event for polishing the practice of mindfulness. All it takes is moving from autopilot mode to a mode of awareness. Learn to be the witness of your considerations and feelings. Get mindful of the foundation, "static" of conventional obviousness, and how seldom you are quiet inside yourself. By watching your feelings and the good and bad times of life, you figure out how to surf the waves. Underneath the surface of the waves are the placidness, quality, and vitality of the universe, which will settle everything in your life.

MINDFULNESS CAN BE ACHIEVED in everyday life by incorporating simple activities like

- While brushing your teeth, feel the touch of the brush on your gums, the taste and scent of toothpaste and the coolness of the water when you flush your mouth.
- When consuming, feel the composition of the sustenance in your mouth and the different flavours and fragrances. Don't ponder on different things or talk, and don't contemplate your next nibble until you have relished the current one totally.
- When conversing with somebody, truly listen

and hear what they are stating without passing judgment on them, considering different things, or arranging what you need to say next.

Mindfulness of the state of being aware is a cumulative result of simple day to day events and your total involvement in each one of them.

3

HOW TO PRACTICE MINDFULNESS

There is an anecdote about a 43-year-old man who was under care after a few hospitalizations and received medication for anxiety-related midsection ache and overpowering anxiety. He reported "I didn't have one good encounter all week." The specialist asked, "Do you shower before work?" The man replied, "Consistently." The advisor inquired as to whether he delighted in showering and the man replied, "A whole lot". "Thus, you do have charming encounters consistently," said the specialist. The man replied, "You mean those little encounters also count?"

MINDFULNESS OBLIGES WITHDRAWING consideration from the past and the future at whatever point they are not required. Your psyche has a tendency to escape the present into the future and the past, which are both illusory. What's to come is either envisioned to be preferred over or more awful than the present. Your past is a history of great and awful encounters, which are not the present moment. To be free of time is to be free of the mental need of the past for your personality and the future for your fulfilment.

Do you talk and ponder on the past? Assuming this is the case, you are not living in the present. Your past and your future are not you, right now. By not dragging the past into each minute, you come back to the minute in which you are currently living. When concentrating on the present, be mindful of time as it is required to perform objectives. On the off chance that you set an objective and move in the direction of it, you are incidentally mindful of time, yet your center is on the present. On the other hand, if you set an objective and concentrate on the objective, the present is simply a going stone to the future and the present loses its natural value.

Managing Thoughts, Reactions and Emotions

Life has cycles of pleasurable moments and terrible nightmares. When we rehearse mindfulness in the event that something makes us furious or harms us, we stop quickly to watch the moment. We turn into the witness of the circumstances and get mindful of our responses. By taking a gander at things in a non-judgmental manner, we detract the force from the circumstances and don't let it sustain our feelings. For instance, on the off chance that you get cut off while travelling in a high traffic situation, instead of responding with street fierceness, essentially watch the cars cut you off, feel your annoyance, and hold up to see what happens next. The displeasure will hit a crest and after that dissolve by surfing the feeling and viewing it without judgment.

"Surrender" is the straightforward alternative to contradicting the stream of, life. Acknowledge the "now." By tolerating the circumstances and making positive moves, we are more successful than by opposing the circumstances and taking negative or no action. In awful or horrendous circumstances, we can make a strategy, or when there is no hope, we can plan. But, this planning must not comprise anticipating the future and running "mental films" that cause us to dismiss the present. If we can't make any move or can't expel ourselves from the circumstances, we must go deeper into surrender, without surrendering. There must never be any imperviousness to actuality. Change frequently occurs with practically no movement at all by going all the more profoundly into the present.

PESSIMISM IS INTERNAL SAFETY, and this safety is negativity. Negativity can't change actuality, but it prevents alluring conditions from happening. We must recognize the pessimism and internal safety and attempt to drop it. Mental and physical strains emerge when there is safety. The free stream of vitality through our body is confined and our wellbeing endures. We make our own particular issues and ache with this pessimism. In the event that we can't drop it, we should either center consideration on it, or get transparent to permit whatever is irritating us to pass through us. As opposed to responding with protection or strike, offer no safety. This doesn't mean you turn into a doormat and endure the awful conduct of others or acknowledge circumstances that are not positive. On the contrary, it implies that they lose their control over you.

MANAGING **Problems**

We bear numerous loads in the psyche. We envision things that may happen later on. When we are brimming with past and future issues, there is no space for new solutions. We can decide to dispose of this trouble by concentrating on the one thing we can do immediately, holding up. There are two sorts of holding up:

1. Small-scale holding up -

This includes things like car influxes or the line at the market or hangar. These are extraordinary open doors for mindfulness, where we can watch the things and individuals around us, and our own particular feelings, as opposed to getting restless. The actuality is, we are holding up, and we must hold up.

1. Large-scale holding up –

It is waiting for a greater house, a compelling relationship, achievement, or the next raise. Some individuals use their entire life holding up in light of the fact that they need the future, not the present. Genuine success is completely tolerating our present actuality and appreciating what we have.

Managing Emotional Turmoil

When we are not aware of the present, each event that induces emotional pain abandons a deposit of torment that lives on in us. This amassed agony is negative vitality that involves our body and brain. It might be torpid, or it could be dynamic. In some individuals, this past agony is dynamic for up to 100% of the time with the result that they live completely in torment. Other individuals might just encounter past agony in specific circumstances, connections, or when it is initiated by a blameless comment or a thought. These painful moments can lead to negative, awful, or self-ruinous musings, practices or sentiments.

It is best to get hold of the past event that causes emotional turmoil at the exact minute it stirs from its torpid state and feel its vitality. Be totally mindful of it. When you do this, the torment loses its control over you. On the off chance that we relate to it, it can assume control over us, get to be some piece of us, and survive inside us. Don't battle this agony. Simply watch it and acknowledge it as what it is in the moment. People looking for salvation later on are attempting to escape some torment. On the off chance that they concentrate on the present, they experience their agony, which they fear. This dissolves the pain affecting you from the past.

Managing Tormenting Relationships

When we encounter tormenting feelings on seeing someone, we typically see that person to be the reason for those sentiments. We project our sentiments outward and assault the other individual. Individuals depend on connections, pills, nourishment, and liquor to conceal their agony. At the point when these things are not accessible or when they quit living up to expectations, the pain is uncovered. In actuality, it is not that person who is causing agony to us, it is us. We have permitted it to happen to us. We must face the agony that is in us instead of attempting to escape it by accusing others. At exactly that point, our agony will break down into the past.

Managing Physical Conditions

Disease and physical ache are an integral part of one's

life. It is proposed not to mark ailment on the grounds that that provides for its actuality, strength, and congruity in time. By standing up to ache and sickness, even demise, just in the present, it is diminished to one or a few of these elements: physical torment, shortcoming, uneasiness, or handicap. Surrender to these variables, not to the thought of illness. We should not accuse ourselves, feel blameworthy, or accuse our lives of its unfairness. The majority of that is the feeling of resistance.

In the event that we get to be genuinely sick and feel furious at these proposals, it is evidence that the ailment has gotten to have become a part of our feeling of self and that we are guarding our character and the illness. Our diseases have nothing to do with who we really are. Surrender to the minute and it will change you. Fear and torment won't essentially be changed into bliss, yet they will be changed into a profound acknowledgement that surpasses straightforward feelings.

4

STEPS TO MINDFULNESS

This chapter includes some steps to mindfulness and some tips for living in the moment. However, these steps must be incorporated with a feeling of gratitude. You should be thankful for all that you have. The fact that you can eat, walk, contemplate and concentrate is the reason why you should be thankful. Mindfulness is a way by which you can connect not only with your own self, but with the whole world as well. The act of living in the present shall leave you happier and healthier.

Breathing

It is said that on the off chance you need to spare yourself thousands in psychologist charges, then you must figure out how to breathe properly. The breath is a great spot to begin. We are breathing constantly, if typically unknowingly. By tuning in, we can bring together, our brain and body, and attach ourselves to the present minute.

You can truly feel strain and anxiety coasting endlessly. Feel the breath coming into your body through the tips of your nostrils and after that leaving your body once more. Take a stab at imagining your breath as a loop. Imagine the breaths in topping off a large portion of the loop then streaming specifically into the breaths out. It is a persistent movement. At whatever point you recognize your brain has meandered, you must bring it again to the breath.

In the event that you need to take it above and beyond, on your breathe-in imagine white mending light entering your body and on your breathe-out imagine tension and strain leaving your body.

Awareness of Your Bodily Sensations

We typically live in our heads and totally disregard our body unless we are in pain. We imagine that our psyche is totally separate from our physical body. To get mindful of your body, send your breath to diverse parts and recognize those body parts. Notice the shivering in your fingers, discharge the anxiety in your stomach, get mindful of the highest point of your head, and feel the pressure in your neck. Getting mindful of your body will bring you into the present minute. It will tweak your faculties and calm the psyche. A great spot to work on tuning in to your body is in the shower. Give careful consideration to the inclination of the water moving over each part of your body, the sensations and the temperature. Bring yourself into complete physical mindfulness.

Concentration on your Mindfulness

Fixation is truly the basis of practicing mindfulness successfully. After everything, you can just practice to the degree that your psyche is smooth. Without focus, your brain will be similar to an uneven ocean in a storm. Consider focus like steady consideration on one thing. It is the measure of time that we can stay centered before we recognize that our psyche has meandered. You must only do one thing at a time. Gradually and deliberately, bring reason into your activities and get mindful of your considerations, movements and particularly your breath.

On the off chance that you are checking your email, simply check your email. You should not bob into Facebook in the meantime. On the other hand, if you are consuming supper, simply consume supper, don't check your telephone and watch the news as well. Each time you perceive your focus has meandered, bring yourself back to focus on your breath. This won't happen overnight. However, with practice, you will get it. The deeper your focus is, the deeper you can enter into mindfulness and its profits.

Mindful Eating

This includes taking a seat at a table and consuming a feast without participating in any other exercises - no daily paper, book, TV, radio, music, or talking. Just consume your dinner, giving careful consideration to which bit of food you select to consume, how it looks, how it smells, how you cut the food, the muscles you use to raise it to your mouth, the surface and taste of the food item as you bite it gradually. You may be stunned at how distinctive food tastes when consumed along these lines and how filling a feast can be. This method of eating is also useful for the digestion process.

Mindful Walking

While strolling, you must focus on the feel of the ground under your feet and your breathing. Simply watch what is around you as you walk and stay in the present. Release your inhibitions and take a gander at the sky, the perspective, and other walkers. Feel the wind, the temperature on your skin and feel delighted in the minute.

UNDERSTAND That You Aren't Your Thoughts and Emotions

A key to mindfulness is the comprehension that your psyche is encountering numerous influences. We generally aren't even mindful that it is occurring. When you comprehend that your brain prattles away, you can avoid letting each thought disturb your inner peace. This is the place where enormous profits begin to happen. You are NOT your sentiments, and you are NOT your considerations.

When you say, "I am disturbed," do you truly imply that you are feeling? If we were our sentiments or considerations, when they vanish, we ought to vanish as well. But we don't. Thoughts, emotions, and feelings blur away. We can additionally prevent them from advancing by changing our considerations. Your sentiments are similar to a climate framework passing through. They are not you.

GET Adequate Sleep

We need slumber to revive our brains and bodies. It is just as simple as this. When we are tired, we can erratically hop from errand to assignment without any genuine clarity. We wind up treading a tiring loop of ceaseless errands. It is an interconnected round, the old chicken or the egg philosophizing. We require mindfulness to sleep, and we need slumber to practice mindfulness. Awful rest propensities damage our bodies. Like a motor without an oil transform, we begin to break down.

Meditation

Meditation opens an entirely new world. You have to turn off your psyche. Your mind does a lot of considering, and we generally aren't even mindful that it is occurring. At the same time, these considerations are influential, and now and again musings can wind into upsetting, negative contemplations and control us. By viewing your brain, you can avoid urges and negative considerations, and you can lead a life free of stress.

Patience

Our brain is extremely anxious and fretful. When we start a mindfulness drill, we create tolerance each time we stop and practice. Keep in mind that everything comes in its own particular time. It's like cooking an egg. If you attempt to hurry it, the yolk will break and make a huge mess. It's especially important to take a gander at your own particular quietness when resentment emerges.

Realize that mindfulness is a practice that can take years to ace. When you first start and you find that your brain is ricocheting from thought to thought, don't be excessively hard on yourself. Create the persistence to realize that it will come in time. Getting eager with a mindfulness practice is just going to back off your progression

Interconnectedness

Everything is associated with everything else. Without daylight, there is no life, without water there is no life, without trees there is no oxygen. It is a complex web of finely adjusted interconnections. It is extremely hazardous to imagine that we exist separately from everything else. Nothing is permanent and the only thing constant is change. This is a fact that can help you in appreciating your circumstances, relationships, and belongings. Each and every thing that you come in contact with is your connection to the world. However, every connection is temporary. Therefore, it should be appreciated for the time that it is there. Mindfulness allows you to discover the different threads of interconnections and give you a broader picture of life.

OTHER MINDFULNESS TECHNIQUES TO **Practice**

Mindfulness has been depicted as a state of being in the present, tolerating things for what they are, i.e. in a non-judgmental manner. It was initially created to help in temperament regulation and backslide aversion and in despondency. It has been found to have respectable well-being profits. Some day-to-day activities that can be useful for achieving mindfulness are –

One Minute Exercise:

Observe a clock or watch. Your undertaking is to center your whole consideration on your breathing, and nothing else, for the moment. Have a go - do it now.

Exercise for De-stressing:

You must choose an erect stance and at that point ask yourself: "What is happening with me right now?" You essentially permit yourself to watch whatever happens. Name any contemplations that you have and afterward allow them to sit, unbothered. Simply be ready to give them a chance to buoy away. Breathe in your surroundings. At the point when feelings or memories of frightful occasions happen, don't permit your own self to wind up. Provide for them short names, for example, "that is a dismal feeling," or "that is a furious feeling," and afterward simply permit them to float or buoy away. These memories and emotions will bit by bit diminish in force and recurrence. Soon you will start to distinguish yourself as a destination eyewitness or witness instead of an individual who is irritated by these considerations and sentiments.

Breathing Exercise:

Stay with any troubling musings for a couple of minutes. Then, as you give them a chance to buoy away, tenderly redirect your full attention to relaxing. Give careful consideration to every breath finished and done as they musically take after one after the other. This will ground you in the present and help you to move into a state of mindfulness and self-awareness.

BASICS OF MINDFUL MEDITATION

Practicing mindful meditation is a pledge that numerous oppose, yet it requires far less time and exertion than most individuals believe it does. The time of the day isn't critical; the customary practice is. In a perfect world, it ought to be rehearsed for 20 to 30 minutes twice a day in a calm room with a shut entryway with no preoccupations. You may want to begin by doing 10 minutes once a day rather than pointing for the "perfect" objective and afterward feeling overwhelmed by it and missing the mark.

Utilize a clock to guarantee that you ruminate as long as you arranged. In the meanwhile, it is beneficial to look for a peaceful and tranquil place, for example, taking a seat in your office or sitting in your auto, getting primed to drive home from the exercise center after your everyday workout. Once more, pick a period when diversions will be negligible. This chapter illustrates one of the most popular methods of performing this form of meditation.

Step 1 –

The first step for any form of meditation is to get into the right posture. You must sit in such a manner that your legs are crossed. Besides this, you must use a meditation pad for a better and more convenient meditation session. You may also choose to sit with your legs broadened straight out or to sit in a seat with a firm back, keeping your feet on the floor and your spine straight, and tucking in your button marginally to keep your vertebrae adjusted appropriately. On the off chance that you have any back, pelvic, or neck ache, back help is fundamental. Indeed, you may need to rest, with your head propped up at a 45-degree angle. In case you're sitting up, close your eyes. If you're lying down, keep your eyes half open to keep yourself from nodding off.

Step 2 –

Focus your eyes. With your eyes shut, center them on one spot, conceivably around the tip of your nose or on your "third eye" (the chakra, or vitality point amidst the eyebrow). On the other hand, turn straight ahead toward the internal parts of your eyelids. As an alternative, you may also choose to roll your eyeballs upward. Whichever eye position you pick, make certain it feels good and that your eye muscles are loose. In the event that you have elevated uneasiness or reasons for alarm, you may need to open your eyes partially or even completely, turning straight ahead toward a spot on the divider or out the window at a stationary item, with a specific end goal to suppress those sentiments. An alternate thought is to close your eyes, and envision being in a spot where you generally feel loose, protected and secure.

Step 3 –

Pay regard to your convenience. With your eyes shut or part of the way open, focusing them on one spot, breathe in with consciousness of your lungs and your stomach. As you breathe in, say to yourself, "In." Exhale from your lungs and afterward your mid-region, saying to yourself, "Out." Do this each one time as you relax. You can additionally utilize the words "climbing" and "falling ceaselessly," or "solace" and "giving up," or "surrender" and "discharge."

Step 4 –

Place your hands in an unwinding and animating mudra (hand position). In Buddhism, the mudra, or position of the hands, in meditation is imperative, on the grounds that it influences the stream of vitality all around the body. There are three customary mudras. Likely the most prevalent one is to touch the thumb and first finger to one another, and after that hold your palms up, with your different fingers loose and straight, and rest the backs of your hands on your thighs.

Step 5 –

Be mindful! As you breathe, rationally note the musings, sentiments, sounds, tastes, smells, and physical sensations, like tingling, temperature, torment or uneasiness, or emotions of greatness and softness that you encounter. Don't attempt to examine any of what you're noting. Essentially be available, open, and watchful. Watch the nature of sensation in the event that it has one, and arrange it: "greatness in shoulders," "astringent taste," "yard cutter outside," "tormenting contemplated child," etc. Don't investigate this thought or feeling unless it happens more than twice, in which case, inquire as to whether you have to manage it now or after your meditation. On the off chance that it needs to be tended to immediately, permit yourself to be available with that sensation, feeling, or redundant thought without judgment as it blurs away or diminishes in power. Subsequently expound on it in a diary, think about it, or converse with a companion or advocate about it.

Step 6 –

Slowly return to conventional cognizance. Take three long, moderate, full breaths, taking in through your nose and out through your mouth. Rub the palms of your hands together to produce hotness, and place the palms over your eyes and face. Open your eyes and gradually lift your hands far from your face as you come back to mindfulness. Breathe in profoundly and stretch your arms up over your head, with your hands interlocked. Curve gradually to the right and afterward to the left. Do this few times, and after that curve forward to your feet. Consider whether anything of vitality uncovered itself to you. In such a case, expound on it in your diary, ponder it, or just move on.

In case you're envisioning a distressing circumstance in which it will be trying to remain nonreactive, or you'll have to have the capacity to get to your innovativeness more than ordinary, attempt to calendar a meditation session quickly.

5

OBSTACLES TO MINDFULNESS AND HOW TO OVERCOME THEM

Positively living in your "now" isn't simple, yet it is very compensating. The most ideal approach to get up and go on your own way, "without a moment's hesitation," is to comprehend the potential deterrents and plan ahead of time on how you'll manage them.

MINDFULNESS REQUIRES PROGRESSING EXERTION.

Mindfulness takes a great deal of work. However, the fortunate thing is that the more time you drill, the less demanding it gets, and the more cheerful your life gets to be. From the start, your musings will be in bedlam, and everything will appear to be crazy. Your circumstance will feel vulnerable. But the more you concentrate on being where you are completely, the simpler it will be to discover true serenity in the given moment and time. Mindfulness is best accomplished when it is practiced throughout the day. It's not only for when you take a seat and contemplate. Concentrate on being aware of your contemplations when you're doing ordinary assignments and it will be simpler to stay mindful when things get extreme.

There will be diversions.

When you're on your excursion to getting more aware of your own self, it appears to be as though the universe begins tossing stuff at you simply to provide you challenges. The preoccupations could be issues throughout your life, show in your connections, or old negative convictions popping up from your past. These are incredible open doors to practice living in the moment. They will help you in becoming stronger, better, and all the more in tune with yourself. The issues and difficulties we face are, in actuality, educators. They are there to help you to develop and to acknowledge who you actually are.

Advancement doesn't generally come rapidly.

Advancement may appear to be excruciatingly abated. There will be times when you join to things and circumstance that you need, which will make it troublesome to be completely in the moment. It's difficult to be careful when you're failing to move on or fixating on what's to come. We all do those things some of the time. I've encountered it endless times in my own life. The more I need something, the more I focus on not having it and needing to get it. When I discharge the connection and concentrate on being thankful for what I already have, my life appears to shift, and advancement appears to happen regularly.

You may need to surrender.

Like with any beneficial adventure, you will have a craving for surrendering and giving up numerous times. It is through these times that you feel most baffled that you are nearly a leap forward. Our lives are very similar to the seasons. We experience chilly, dull winters, and upbeat, stretching summers. Everything goes back and forth. It's the rhythmic movement of life. When you understand that the testing times are there to help you develop, you will naturally feel more quiet and loose.

Your objectives may challenge **your mindfulness.**

Having objectives is phenomenal, key even, yet when you get to be excessively connected to them, something terrible happens. You realize that you're over-attached when you begin feeling baffled, furious, and negative. Connection tangles our clarity. You are seeking after your objectives on the grounds that you accept that they will make you euphoric. Keep that in mind when you begin letting your objectives pull you into an upsetting state of psyche. On the off chance that you concentrate on the great things around you, you'll feel that satisfaction that you think you have to pursue. This will make you much more content in the long haul, and, obviously, at this time.

You may overlook **that the journey is the goal.**

Most individuals miss the fact that the fun of a journey is not in the destination, but in the journey itself. Have you ever perceived that when you achieve an objective, it is not as energizing as you thought it would be? Of course, it feels incredible to hit a turning point, but in the event that you don't supplant that objective with another, you will soon end up feeling unfulfilled. People need objectives so they can have a feeling of reason and satisfaction. It is in during the adventure that we learn, develop, and get better.

When you're honing mindfulness, recollect that there is no place to touch base. In the event that you concentrate on what is going on at this time, the rest will deal with itself. Indeed the most edified experts on earth need to manage troublesome circumstances and disorganized musings. The distinction is that they have figured out how to acknowledge the minute for what it is. When you do this, you turn into the gatekeeper of your internal space, which is the best way to feel great inside and discover significant serenity at this moment.

www.ingramcontent.com/pod-product-compliance
Lightning Source LLC
Chambersburg PA
CBHW052129110526
44592CB00013B/1814